Boston Terrier

By Ann McCammon

BREEDERS' BEST™

A KENNEL CLUB BOOK®

BOSTON TERRIER

ISBN: 1-59378-939-X

Copyright © 2005

Kennel Club Books, LLC
308 Main Street, Allenhurst, NJ 07711 USA
Printed in South Korea

PHOTOS BY:
Isabelle Français
and Paulette Braun.

DRAWINGS BY:
Yolyanko el Habanero

Contents

CHAPTER **1**

Meet the Boston Terrier

Perpetually dressed in a dapper tuxedo, the Boston Terrier has truly earned the nickname "American Gentleman."

T he Boston Terrier is considered to be a true American breed, as its beginnings trace back to the city of Boston in the great state of Massachusetts. With his sparkling "bib and tucker" markings, he looks every inch a true American gentleman. Are you looking for a small-sized "below-the-knee" dog, one that is lively and has personality plus? A dog that requires a minimum of grooming and that is considered a fairly "easy keeper"? If so, the Boston Terrier may be just the dog for you!

The early Boston Terriers, in the last half of the 19th century, were fairly hefty dogs, looking somewhat like the present-day American Staffordshire Terrier. The dogs in the background of the first Boston Terriers were the Bull Terrier, the English Bulldog and the White English Terrier, which is now extinct. In time, there were even crosses to the French Bulldog. The early breeders were interested in a dog that had the toughness of the two "bully" breeds but that would also have the quickness of the terrier.

As American as Uncle Sam is Boston's own contribution to the pure-bred dog world.

The original dogs were good-sized, weighing close to 30 pounds, and they were bred by the Irishmen of Boston who owned the livery stables. This was a lively group of men who used to hang out at John Barnard's kennels on Myrtle Street, where the pros and cons of the various "Roundheads" were discussed. At this time, the purpose of breeding the so-called Roundheads was to develop a better, tougher and quicker dog for the

Short-coated, compact in size and huge in personality, it's no wonder that the Boston Terrier has experienced sky-high popularity through the years.

popular pastime of dog fighting. By the turn of the 20th century, this bloody sport thankfully was banned, and the Boston Terrier became a companion dog for the family to enjoy.

In 1878, the breed was entered for the first time at the New England dog show held in Boston. Since there were no classes for the breed, the dogs were entered in the class for Bull Terriers. By 1888, Boston Terriers finally had their own class for entries, but they were called "Round-headed Bull Terriers, any color." Entries were high, and the class became permanent at the shows, thereby giving the Boston Terrier the name of "Roundhead" or "Boston Roundhead."

By 1891, the American Bull Terrier Club (which was a club made up of Boston Terrier fanciers) had applied for admission into the American Kennel Club (AKC) stud book, but had run into opposition because of the name of the

breed and the lack of consistency in breeding programs with the crosses to the Bulldog and terriers. Discussions took place over a two-year period, and it was decided that, since the birthplace of the dog was Boston, the breed would become known as the Boston Terrier. In 1893, the application was resubmitted and accepted by the AKC, and the national club, the Boston Terrier Club of America, was formed. There were about 75 dogs accepted into the stud book, as these dogs had been certified as having been bred pure for at least three generations. These dogs became the foundation of the breed in America and beyond.

In 1916, Ch. Hagerty King was whelped. Experts consider this dog to be the best of the bull-and-terrier crosses, and he was the best specimen yet seen of a Boston. He was purchased by his owner for $2,500, a tremendous amount of money for the day, and quite a hefty sum still today! He was used briefly at stud and sired five champions. The breed rapidly gained in popularity after this date and by 1934 the AKC had registered 90,000 Bostons. Prices soared, with a puppy from top breeding stock bringing up to $150 and stud services costing as much as $100. By this time, there were some outstanding stud dogs being used for breeding, and the present-day type of Boston Terrier was set.

As the 20th century progressed, the Boston became so popular that the breed often made up more than 20% of the entries at an all-breed dog show, and it was not unusual to have a specialty show entry of 200 dogs. Between 1920 and 1960, the Boston was always in the top ten most popular breeds in the US (according to AKC registration statistics); during many of those years, it held the number one or two position. The breed still remains in the top 20 AKC registered breeds.

Many of the best-known all-around judges, those who are able to judge all AKC breeds, started their dog careers with the Boston Terrier. These include such dog-world legends as Vincent Perry, Alva Rosenberg, Marie Ferguson and Ray Perso, all deceased now but

Stocky, wide-eyed and absolutely irresistible, Boston pups are easy to fall in love with.

whose breeding programs surely left a large mark upon the breed. Vincent Perry, of Globe Glowing Kennels, considered to be one of the great dog men of the 20th century, was active in the breed up until the time of his death in 1985. His dogs sired many champions and surely made an impact upon the breed in the first half of the century.

The Boston Terrier over the years has been somewhat exceptional in having extremely dedicated breeders who stayed with the breed and who were always striving to breed better dogs. Some of them in the mid-20th century were Harry Clasen, Byron Munson, Cora Brat and Leonard Myers, to mention just a few of the greats.

By the 1970s, new and younger breeders came upon the scene and added more great dogs to the gene pool and center ring. Betty Swick of KimKev Kennels in Colorado owned Bostons for 60 years and bred many champions and top show winners. Bob and Eleanor Candland, from California, bred, owned and handled Ch. El-Bo's Rudy Is a Dandy, who won 16 all-breed Bests in Show and sired 58 champions. Bob Breum, from Omaha, Nebraska, owned Ch. Zodiac's Special Beau, who was considered to be one of the best-showing and best-

Boston Terriers are delightful companion dogs who enjoy the comforts of home with families all over the US and around the world.

producing Bostons of his time. Beau won ten all-breed Bests in Show and sired 41 champions, of which five were Top Ten winners. Michael and Beverly Staley bred and owned Ch. Staley's El-Bo's Showman, who won multiple Bests in Show and sired at least 75 champions. Many other breeders, too many to mention here, made considerable contributions to this great breed. At the present time, there are many newer and younger breeders on the scene who are also producing exceptional dogs.

Throughout the years, the Boston Terrier has remained a favorite with the public. Its popularity, although not as extreme as it was in past decades, still remains high. This is a breed that continues to be dearly loved by the public, and many people who grew up with Boston Terriers wouldn't think of betraying their beloved Roundheads for another breed.

MEET THE BOSTON TERRIER

Overview

- The Boston Terrier is an American original, with its roots in Boston, Massachusetts.
- The breed can trace its ancestry back to bully breeds and terriers, with breeders hoping to create a quick, tough fighting dog. As years passed, the breed became a lover, not a fighter!
- Nicknamed "Roundheads," Boston Terriers had a devoted band of fanciers who formed a club and lobbied for AKC recognition. There have been many influential breeders and dogs who were instrumental in the breed's establishment.
- Over the course of its history, the Boston Terrier has been one of the most popular dogs in the US, with high registration numbers. It still is among the top AKC-registered breeds in the country.

Are You a Boston Terrier Person?

You don't need to live in the 02110 zip code area to own a Boston Terrier. This is a breed that finds itself at home almost anywhere. Here's an adaptable, affable fellow who's not averse to a game of football, a rowdy tea party or a nice stroll downtown. All in all, the Boston Terrier is a companion dog—and that is considered to be his only job! This means that he has been bred to have an even disposition and that he is a small dog who finds that his primary occupation in life is to keep his owners happy.

Inquisitive, alert and just plain charming, the Boston Terrier is fun to spend time with.

Even though he's a smallish companion dog, he's no toy dog—he's bigger than you think, and heavy for his size. Despite the "Terrier" in his name, he's not categorized at dog shows as a Terrier. In fact, at shows in the US, he competes in the Non-Sporting Group; in England, he belongs to the Utility Group. He finds himself classed with other terrific companion dogs like the Bichon Frise, Chow Chow, Shiba Inu and Miniature and Standard Poodles. He is considered to be a small- to medium-sized dog, weighing no more than 25 pounds in the largest weight class and weighing less than 15 pounds in the smallest weight class according to AKC specifications.

And we thought the Boston wasn't a "toy" dog.

Before purchasing your Boston, you must give some thought to the personality and characteristics of this dog to determine if this is the breed for you. There are many considerations before you purchase any dog.

Thinking deep thoughts! The Boston Terrier is a delightful mix of intelligence, devotion to his family and outgoing nature.

Let's begin with the most obvious question: do you have the time to give to a dog? He will need care, companionship, training and grooming. This is almost like having a child, except the dog remains childlike and will always require your care, though he doesn't strain your bank account when college time rolls around. No matter what the hardcore purists say, you *can* work a full-time job and own a dog. It's just a matter of setting priorities and including your Boston Terrier in your life when you're not in the office or on the job.

Nowadays owners have many options, including pet-sitters, dog-walkers and, best of all, doggy daycare! Your Boston Terrier will need quality time, though, just as a child needs it. He must be fed on a regular schedule and exercised several times a day. Consider taking him to the dog park or to some other dog-friendly location that your Boston will enjoy. Regardless of where you're going, he will likely enjoy rides in the car with you.

A well-"dressed" bunch in their black-and-white finery, enjoying some relaxation time outdoors.

In addition to just spending time together, you must work with him to have an obedient dog that has good manners. You must devote time to his training and also make sure that he gets sufficient activity to keep him happily occupied. A walk or a good romp, in the morning and again in the evening, is the minimum.

Although grooming is minimal with the Boston, he will need to have his coat brushed on a regular basis and to have his toenails trimmed, teeth brushed and eyes and ears kept clean. You will want to make sure that he is a tidy dog that smells good.

Is this your first dog? Boston Terriers may not be the best dogs for first-time owners, though they tend to be popular choices for these well-intentioned novices. This is a smart dog who needs an owner that is equally as smart as, or smarter than, he is.

Doggy smarts are acquired mainly through experience, but reading this book from cover to cover is a good start in your Boston education.

"Hey, can you give me a lift?" Well-socialized Bostons should be friendly toward other dogs as well as other kinds of pets.

When deciding to purchase a dog, remember that you are adding a member to your family and another four feet to your home. The Boston Terrier certainly is a companion that must live in the house with you and that will want to spend his waking hours with the family. Although Bostons aren't as needy as some spoiled toy dogs, they do require and thrive on human companionship. Are you ready to share your life with this handsome fellow?

Beyond these considerations, let's think about the kids. Do you have small children and are you willing to teach and supervise them so that they will not mistreat this pet? The Boston, because of his smallish size, will not handle any mistreatment from a child. Unlike a Boxer or a Golden Retriever, which will tolerate a certain amount of

Smooch! No matter what you're doing, there's always time to take a break and show your affectionate Boston how much you love him.

rough-and-tumble from a child, the Boston could have severe damage done to him through mishandling. You will have to teach your children how to behave toward and around the family pet.

Another consideration is your outdoor accommodations: do you have a fenced-in yard for your Boston? This is not a breed that you can leave tied out on the porch. Even though he is a small dog, he must have a secure area in which to run and exercise. A fenced yard should give you ample space to throw a ball and your dog freedom to run around as he pleases.

Perhaps the most obvious concern is financial. Can you afford to own and care for a dog? Beyond the initial expense of the puppy, which is a drop in the bucket compared to the expenses involved over the lifetime of the dog, there are the costs for veterinary care (inoculations, check-ups, pet insurance, medication, etc.), basic equipment (like collars, leads, bowls, flea and heartworm preventives, brushes and clippers, etc.), accommodations (a crate, a bed, a fence) and of course food, which can be costly. There's also the expense of boarding the dog if you go on vacation or the weekly cost of doggy daycare or a dog walker if you are working a 9 to 5 job. Another potential expense is an air conditioner, if you don't already have one, since Bostons can overheat in the summer months and can experience breathing difficulties in hot, humid weather.

The Boston is dearly loved for his disposition, his size and his good looks. In addition, he is loved for his intelligence, his devotion to his family, his liveliness and his alert nature. However, do learn about the breed before rushing out and buying the first puppy you see. An excellent source of information is available on the Internet at www.bostonterrier-clubofamerica.org, the website of the national breed club, the Boston Terrier Club of America.

ARE YOU A BOSTON TERRIER PERSON?

Overview

- The Boston's only job is to be a wonderful companion. He's loyal, friendly and intelligent, a great choice for dog owners with "doggie smarts."
- The Boston is a relatively small dog, with a short coat and short muzzle. His grooming needs are minimal, but owners must take precautions that these short-faced dogs do not overheat and be aware of potential breathing problems.
- The Boston thrives on his family's attention and companionship. You must be prepared to spend time with your Boston, training him, doing activities with him and making him a true part of your life and home.
- Do you know what it takes to care for a Boston, or any dog for that matter? Is your entire family ready? Do you have time for a dog, as well as money for healthcare, supplies, etc.?

CHAPTER 3

The Boston Terrier Standard

Every breed of dog registered with the American Kennel Club (AKC) has a standard, a document that gives a detailed description of what the breed should look and act like. The Boston Terrier standard was formulated by the breed's parent club, the Boston Terrier Club of America (BTCA), and you can find the complete standard on the AKC's website, www.akc.org. The Boston Terrier is a lively, sturdy, intelligent and confident dog that is also

The Boston Terrier's slightly arched neck contributes to his elegant and dignified head carriage.

16

very affectionate, devoted, loyal and, of course, very loving. You will never find him boring, as his lively dark button eyes will show that he is game for anything! He is a well-balanced dog with a head that is in proportion to his size. His colors are either brindle, seal or black, all colors being evenly marked with white. The standard notes that "the dog conveys an impression of determination, strength and activity, with style of a high order; carriage easy and graceful."

The breed's alert intelligence shows in a curious expression that says, "Tell me more!"

According to the AKC standard, there are three weight classes for the Boston: under 15 pounds; 15 pounds and under 20 pounds; 20 pounds, not to exceed 25 pounds. He should be square in appearance and should not look either blocky or chunky. His expression, which is very important, is alert and kind, indicating a high degree of intelligence. His ears are small and carried erect.

This is a breed that's as playful as he is smart—he has a goofy side and a real zest for life.

CHAPTER 3

Skull: Cranium.

Stop: Indentation between eyes at point of nasal bones and skull.

Muzzle: Foreface or region of head in front of eyes.

Lip: Fleshy portion of upper and lower jaws.

Occiput: Upper back part of skull; apex

Topline: Outline from withers to tailset.

Withers: Highest part of back, at the base of neck above shoulders.

Shoulder: Upper point of forequarters; region of the two shoulder blades.

Forechest: Sternum.

Forequarters: Front assembly from shoulder to feet.

Chest: Thoracic cavity (enclosed by ribs).

Upper arm: Region between shoulder blade and forearm.

Brisket: Lower chest.

Elbow: Region where upper arm and forearm meet.

Forearm: Region between elbow and wrist.

Carpus: Wrist.

Dewclaw: Extra digit on inside of leg; fifth toe.

Pastern: Region between wrist and toes.

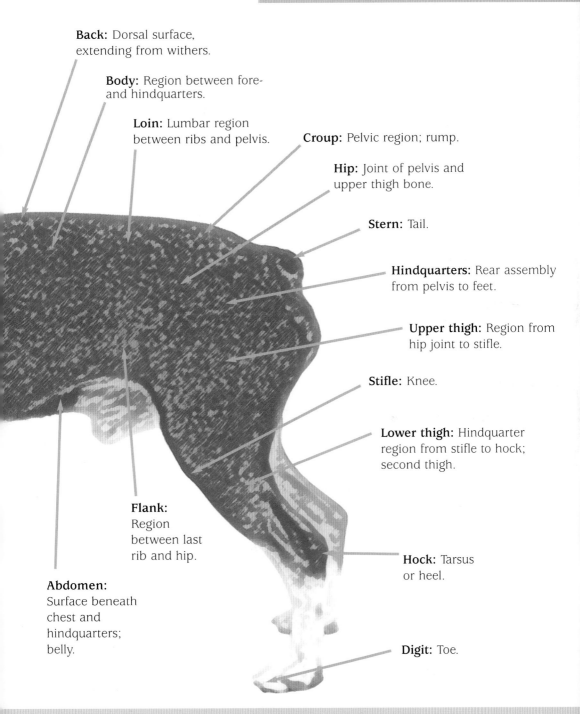

Back: Dorsal surface, extending from withers.

Body: Region between fore- and hindquarters.

Loin: Lumbar region between ribs and pelvis.

Croup: Pelvic region; rump.

Hip: Joint of pelvis and upper thigh bone.

Stern: Tail.

Hindquarters: Rear assembly from pelvis to feet.

Upper thigh: Region from hip joint to stifle.

Stifle: Knee.

Lower thigh: Hindquarter region from stifle to hock; second thigh.

Flank: Region between last rib and hip.

Abdomen: Surface beneath chest and hindquarters; belly.

Hock: Tarsus or heel.

Digit: Toe.

The Boston has a slightly arched neck, which gives him a very graceful appearance. His topline is level and his thighs are strong and well muscled. He should have small, compact feet

We've mentiond that the breed's colors are brindle, seal or black, all with white markings. Seal is described as a coat that appears black but, when in the sunlight, will have

The Boston is a compact, well-muscled dog with a sleek, close-fitting coat.

that turn neither in nor out. The standard notes that "the gait of the Boston Terrier is that of a sure footed, straight gaited dog, forelegs and hind legs moving straight ahead in line with perfect rhythm, each step indicating grace and power."

a red cast. Solid colors without the white markings are unacceptable. White Boston Terriers, sometimes sold by disreputable breeders as "rare" Bostons, are not acceptable in any form. These are dogs that should not be sold and surely should not be purchased by an uninformed buyer.

There are some disqualifications in the breed when it comes to showing the Boston. A Dudley nose, which is a flesh-colored nose, is unacceptable. A docked or surgically shortened tail is unacceptable. On occasion, a breeder will sell one of his dogs because the dog does not have the acceptable markings for the show ring. This does not mean that the dog is not well bred and does not carry the acceptable conformation and

temperament of the Boston. It simply means that the breeder is looking for more desirable markings for the dog that he is going to be showing. This Boston should make a great pet.

In closing, the standard notes: "The Boston Terrier is a friendly and lively dog. The breed has an excellent disposition and a high degree of intelligence, which makes the Boston Terrier an incomparable companion." We couldn't have said it better!

THE BOSTON TERRIER STANDARD

Overview

- The AKC's breed standard gives a detailed description of all aspects of the ideal representative of the Boston Terrier breed. Every AKC-recognized breed has such a document.
- Physically, the Boston is a small-sized dog, seen in different weight ranges, with a compact body, graceful head carriage and erect ears.
- Temperamentally, this is a lively, bright, friendly dog, known for his good disposition and prized for his suitability as a companion.
- Along with desirable traits, the standard also lists faults. Some minor faults are small "beauty points" that would prohibit the dog from being shown but have no effect on his companion qualities, while others are more serious flaws.

Selecting a Breeder

You've decided that the Boston is the perfect dog for you. Now it's time to find a breeder. Since Boston Terriers are fairly popular in most states, you should not have much problem locating a breeder who lives within a reasonable distance. Not every breeder and every puppy are created equal. Your best bet is to select a responsible breeder through the Breeder Referral Committee of the Boston Terrier Club of America. The chairperson of the committee provides a list of breeders state by state. These breeders abide by a strict code of ethics and only breed to

Puppies get their best start in life when they come from a carefully planned mating, a dedicated breeder and, of course, a loving mom!

improve the Boston Terrier, using the AKC breed standard as the yardstick of perfection.

You may find a recommended breeder in your own area, or you may have to drive some distance. This is a minor inconvenience, especially if it will lead you to finding a truly excellent puppy that is healthy and sound and that looks and acts like a Boston Terrier.

The pups need to stay with their dam for around the first eight weeks of life. They nurse for their first weeks and, after weaning, are still taught valuable pack lessons by their mom.

Good breeders give considerable thought before breeding their bitches, staying on top of the latest health-screening tests available. A respon-sible breeder is someone who is dedicated to the breed and to breeding out any faults and hered-itary problems and whose overall interest is in improving the breed. In addition to breeding to the standard, the responsible breeder only breeds bitches and dogs that are tested as free of the hereditary problems known in the breed; he should be

With one pup cuter than the next, a litter of tiny tuxedo-clad Boston babies can certainly make it hard for you to choose!

happy to show you this documentation along with the pup's pedigree. There have been many conformationally superb dogs that unfortunately have perpetuated various hereditary problems to future lines of Bostons.

When you visit a top-quality breeder, you will know it from the moment you enter his facility. Many breeders raise their litters in their own kitchens or family rooms, right in the midst of the family, though there are some breeders who have

A Boston Terrier puppy is a tiny creature that represents a huge responsibility. Are you ready?

kennels with whelping rooms and play areas for puppies. A kennel should be clean and temperature-regulated, and the breeder must spend adequate time making sure that the pups get the human contact they need.

Committed breeders "live Bostons." They study pedigrees, know the dogs and the other breeders, visit dog shows and often show their own dogs or participate in other canine activities. Breeders must stay current and must know what the leading stud dogs are producing. When it comes to selecting the right stud dog for his bitch, a breeder may fly the bitch across the country to breed to a particular stud dog, or he may drive the bitch a considerable distance to the dog. He may have only one or two litters each year, which means that there may not be a puppy ready for you when you first call. Further, Bostons have relatively small litters, and there is a puppy fatality factor related to the breed's need for Caesarean sections, so you may be put on a waiting list for a pup if approved by the breeder. Remember that you are purchasing a new family member, so the wait, effort and expense will be well worthwhile.

Part of "living Bostons" is belonging to the national parent club, the BTCA, as well as a local or regional breed club. Breeders typically will belong to these clubs and remain active participants for many years. Check out the BTCA's website for a listing of local Boston Terrier clubs. You should be able to find one in your state or region. Local BTCA-affiliated clubs can also help you in your breeder search. In addition, breed clubs should be able to answer any questions that you may have about owning a Boston Terrier.

The responsible Boston Terrier breeder will probably be someone who has been breeding for some years and someone who is known on

This pile of pups is raised right inside the breeder's home, getting accustomed to the sights, sounds and smells of everyday life in a human pack.

the national level. Participating in club activities, supporting the goals of the club and showing their dogs are ways that breeders gain reputations and further their knowledge.

When it's time to contact a breeder, be clear about your intentions. Be specific about your wants and dislikes, don't be overly fussy (for instance, do not specify brindle, seal or black, since the colors are similar anyway). Since you are likely seeking a pet, not a show dog, tell the breeder that you are seeking a pet Boston. Do not pretend that you're going to show the dog, thinking that you'll get a better puppy. Every puppy that a reputable breeder sells will be healthy, sound and typical of the breed. Do not fret over the lack of a muzzle band or an overblown blaze. Unless the puppy is solid white, there's never too much white on a pet puppy, as long as it's healthy.

Once you have set up an appointment with the breeder, be on time, courteous and relaxed. The breeder will show you his kennel, if he has a kennel, or invite you into his home to see the puppies' quarters.

It can be hard to choose, but when your perfect pup picks you, you will know it!

These areas will be clean and smell good. The breeder will show you the dam of the litter, and she will be clean, good smelling and groomed. The puppies will also be spotless, with trimmed toenails and clean faces. The breeder may show you only the available puppies, as he may not show you the puppies that are already sold or that he is going to keep for showing. The dam should always be on the premises, and if the breeder tells you that the dam is back at her owner's kennel, you should be skeptical. Most breeders do not loan out bitches the way they do stud dogs.

Be ready for a mini-"inquisition" from the breeder, as he's not going to hand you over a puppy as if he's just sold you a used lawnmower or car. He has to approve you as a suitable home for one of his pups. Here are some of the questions you'll encounter—

be honest, as the breeder has the puppy's and your best interests at heart. Have you

Boston females are loving moms, caring for their pups with watchful eyes.

had a dog before? How many have you had and have you ever owned a Boston? Did your dogs live long lives? Do you have a fenced yard? How many children do you have and what are their ages? Are you willing to spend the time to teach your children how to treat the new family member? Will someone be home during the day to care for and train the pup? Have you ever done any dog training and are you willing

CHAPTER 4

to go to obedience classes with your dog? Are there any other pets in your household?

Do not be offended by these questions. If you can't answer these questions easily and honestly, perhaps you're finding out that you're not ready for Boston adoption. The breeder has put a lot of effort and money into this litter, and his first priority is to place the pups in caring and appropriate households where each Boston baby will be wanted, loved and cared for. You should be confident about your ability to accept the responsibility for this dog's well-being for his entire life.

Lastly, consider how you get along with the breeder whom you've selected. You are entering into what should

A good breeder starts evaluating the pups for show potential at a young age, possibly keeping for himself those that he feels are the most promising prospects.

be a long-term relationship with this person, as you will rely on him for advice, assistance and direction over the years to come. The truly great breeders establish a "dog family," a network of Boston owners who rely on the breeder to be the patriarch of the pack. These breeders have many repeat clients who purchase their first dog, their second dog and so on from the same breeder. Nothing could be more comforting than to be adopted by a great breeder who wants to share his precious line with you. When you find a personable, honest and ethical breeder, you will know it, as once he's deemed you a suitable owner, he will welcome you into his Boston fold and entrust you with his Boston kids.

SELECTING A BREEDER

Overview

- A good puppy starts with a good breeder, whether seeking a pet or show puppy. The BTCA has a breeder referral service to help guide prospective owners to a reliable puppy source.
- A good breeder only wants to improve the breed. He takes health, temperament and conformation issues seriously when planning a mating.
- When visiting the litter, you should be comfortable with the breeder and satisfied with the condition of the puppy-raising areas, the litter and the dam.
- Just as you will have many questions for the breeder, he will be just as eager to interrogate you to make sure that you are a worthy owner for one of his pups.
- A relationship with a good breeder is one that can last a lifetime as you become part of his extended Boston family.

Finding the Right Puppy

Finally, the fun begins! What is more exciting than selecting a puppy from a well-bred litter of Bostons! Keep your head, and leave your wallet and your children at home. Knowing that you have located a responsible breeder with an excellent reputation for healthy, sound puppies makes this selection process more fun than effort. Children will be excited to meet the puppies, but they can distract you from the task at hand.

Now, let's talk about sex. Before seeing the breeder and his pups, you

All Boston puppies are adorable, and each one is an individual. You must get to know them beyond that puppy cuteness to decide which one is best for you.

should give some consideration as to whether you prefer a male or a female for a pet. Some individuals consider males easier to train but the more aggressive of the two sexes. Others prefer the softer, more loving disposition of the female. There are several points that should be considered in making your decision. In the Boston Terrier, the size of either sex will make little difference, except that the bitch will be slightly more refined in appearance than the male.

The pup you choose should be friendly and confident, enjoying your attention and comfortable with being held and petted.

Many of the dog's sexual traits will be softened or eliminated by spaying or neutering, which breeders often require of all pet dogs. If for some reason you do not plan to neuter or spay your pet, understand that the female will come into season approximately every six months. This can be a difficult time for up to three weeks, as it is fairly messy and hard on the house, and it will attract any loose

The breeder cares very much that each and every pup finds a wonderful home.

CHAPTER 5

males in the neighborhood, who will sit on your doorstep like lovelorn swains. If you have two opposite-sex Bostons in the house, be assured that your unneutered male will stop eating, mount everything in his path and think about nothing other than perpetu-

have more of a tendency to lift his leg and to mount. Additionally, neutering/spaying has important health benefits for both sexes. If you are not sure which sex you want, discuss it with the breeder and he should be able to help.

When looking over the

A bunch of bubbly Boston babies—much more appealing to find in your basket than a load of laundry!

ating "his race" during the female's heat cycle. Under normal circumstances, the pet male who is not neutered can be more aggressive and will

pups, do not pick the puppy that hangs back—and think twice before picking the extra-active, most outgoing of the litter. However, do keep in mind that all typical Boston puppies will be quite active, some of them even a bit hyper. Off-the-wall puppies can turn into wild adults and will require more patience and time in training. Look for the middle-of-the-road puppy, the one that is interested, comes up to you, listens when you speak and looks very alert. Do not pick the pup that is overly shy and will not approach you. Never pick a puppy because you "feel sorry" for him. Don't forget—you are adding a new member to your family and you want one that is bright, healthy and, of course, fun!

When visiting the litter, you arrive at the appointed time and the breeder has the puppies ready for you to look at. They should be a happy bunch, clean and groomed. Their noses will be wet, their coats will have a glow or sheen and they will have a nice covering of flesh over their ribs. You will be ready to pick up these rascals and cuddle them in your arms. The pups should be easily encouraged to come to you. The breed prides itself on its friendly disposition and lovable character.

You should ask the breeder

The breeder monitors all aspects of the pups' health and development as they grow.

if the sire and dam of the litter have had their temperaments tested. These tests are offered by the American Temperament Test Society (ATTS). A number of breeders are familiar with this organization and have their animals tested. If so, the breeder will show you the score sheets, and you can easily determine if these dogs have the personality you are looking for, which in turn should be evident in the pups. In addition, this is an excellent indication that this is a responsible breeder.

Temperament testing by the ATTS is done on dogs that are at least 18 months of age; therefore puppies are not tested, but the sire and dam can be tested. The test is like a simulated walk through a park or neighborhood where everyday situations are encountered. Neutral, friendly and threatening situations are encountered to assess the dog's reactions to the various stimuli. Problems that are looked for are unprovoked aggression, panic without recovery and strong avoidance. Behavior toward strangers, reaction to auditory, visual and tactile stimuli and self-protective and aggressive behavior are watched for. The dog is on a loose lead for the

test, which takes about ten minutes to complete. Recent statistics show that, out of 50 Bostons tested by the ATTS, 84% had a passing rate, which is high compared to some breeds.

Some breeders will have the temperaments of their puppies tested by either a professional trainer, their veterinarian or another dog breeder. They will find the high-energy pup and the pup that is slower to respond. They will find the pup with the independent spirit and the one that will want to follow the pack. If the litter has had any type of temperament testing, the breeder will use this information to suggest which pup he thinks will be best for your family. Even if no testing has been done, a good breeder will know the pups well enough to guide you in your choice.

If the litter has not been tested, you can do a few simple tests while you are sitting on the floor, playing with the pups. Pat your leg or snap your finger and see which pup comes up to you first. Clap your hands and see if any pups shy away from you. See how they play with one another. Watch for the one that has the most appealing personality to you, as this will probably be the puppy that you will take home. Look for the puppy that appears to be "in the middle," not overly rambunctious, overly aggressive or submissive. You want the joyful pup, not the wild one. Spend some time selecting your puppy and if you are hesitant, tell the breeder that you would like to go home and think over your decision.

Once you have made a preliminary decision, based on the puppy's temperament, overall appearance and health and your gut feeling, tell the breeder which puppy you are leaning toward and then make an appointment to return to make your final choice. This is a major decision, as you are adding a family member who may be with you for 10 to 15 years. Be sure to get the puppy that you will all be happy with.

Snuggling up with Mom is the pups' favorite place to be at this age.

Now's the time to bring the kids and the wallet. You are now ready to select your puppy. If the same puppy appeals to you after some time of dreaming about your new puppy, then you likely have found the Boston Terrier for you. You are ready to become a Boston person and your whole family is ready for this new arrival into your home and lives.

Before we move on to the big arrival, let's consider one other option that you may find attractive, affordable and in many ways easier. There is another way to add a Boston Terrier to your life, and that is to adopt a "rescue" Boston. This will be a dog who, for a wide variety of reasons, needs a new home. This will usually

Support the rescue effort! Adopting an adult rescue Boston is a rewarding way to find a great new companion while helping a dog in need.

be a dog over one year of age and very often trained and housebroken. The breed rescue organization has these dogs checked by vets and kept in foster homes, where they are cared for while awaiting permanent homes. Usually these dogs make marvelous pets, as they are grateful for another chance at a loving home.

The BTCA has a dedicated group of fanciers who work to rescue Bostons. Information about the Boston Terrier rescue groups is available on the BTCA website, including contact information for the major regional groups. Rescue committees consist of very dedicated individuals who care deeply about the breed and give countless hours of their time and money to assure that each dog will have an equal chance in life. Do investigate the background of the dog as much as possible, as you do not want to be taking home the problems that someone else may have instilled in this particular dog. By going through the BTCA's rescue organization, you should be assured of getting a dog that you will be able to live with.

Adopting an adult presents many advantages over the selection of a puppy. Another way to obtain an adult dog is from a breeder, who may have an older dog that he wants to place in a good home. Some breeders place champion dogs in pet homes after these dogs' careers have run their courses. The breeders pride themselves on "retiring" the dogs to good pet homes, where they will receive the optimum of attention. In some cases, these dogs are only four or five years old, in excellent health, well trained and as beautiful as any Boston can be! Do give this some thought, as often an older dog will be much easier to live with than a puppy, and you save a lot of time and money on wee-wee pads, obedience classes and replacing chewed-up shoes!

FINDING THE RIGHT PUPPY

Overview

- Keep your wits about you when selecting your puppy. Think about your intentions and ask the breeder for advice to help you make a wise choice.
- Do you want a male or a female? Pet puppy or show prospect? Communicate your wants honestly to the breeder.
- Observing the litter is fun and informative. See that all pups are healthy and watch them play with you and with each other to assess each one's personality.
- The breeder may do formal temperament testing or will give you advice based on his own experience and observations.
- Have you considered rescuing an adult Boston in need of a home? All the love of a Boston, none of the hassle of a puppy!

37

Welcoming the Boston Terrier

E lectricity is in the air: the puppy comes home today! Short of making a banner that heralds "Welcome Home, Harry!" the puppy's homecoming should be a low-key affair. Try to keep the kids occupied (perhaps with the banner), so that you can Boston-proof the house, buy the accessories and food you need and otherwise prepare yourself for the puppy's arrival.

Before bringing the pup home, you must plan on going shopping for your puppy's accessories. Here's a list of the Boston basics: stainless steel water and food bowls, a light-weight collar and leash, an ID tag,

When you've lost your heart to the Boston, it can be hard to resist owning more than one.

a wire crate and a couple of safe chew toys. The most important item on this list is the dog crate. You should purchase a medium-sized crate for your puppy; he will grow into it. This will be his "den away from home," his retreat when he wants to take a nap, snuggle up to a toy or sleep for the night.

Once your whole family has agreed on the perfect pup, it's time to get ready for his homecoming.

The puppy will welcome the crate not only at night but also at times when he is home alone. In very short order, your puppy will feel safe and secure when he is in the crate. Left uncrated and alone, he will quickly become bored and begin to chew on anything he can find. Keeping him in a confined area when you are out of the house prevents these problems. Be sure to add several towels or a washable blanket to the crate so that he will be comfortable. You will learn that the crate is also your most important house-training tool, one that will save you much aggravation, clean-up time and home repairs.

"Did I just hear you say that I'm the cutest thing you've ever seen?"

You must puppy-proof your house. Boston Terrier pups are naturally curious critters that will investigate everything new, then seek-and-destroy just because it's fun. The message here is: Never let your puppy roam your house or yard unsupervised. Scout your house indoors and out for the following hazards:

Trash Cans and Diaper Pails
These are natural puppy magnets (they know where the good smelly stuff is!).

Medication Bottles, Cleaning Materials, Roach and Rodent Poisons
Lock these up. You'll be amazed at what a determined puppy can find.

Electrical Cords
Unplug them wherever you can and make the others inaccessible. Injuries from chewed electrical cords are extremely common in young dogs.

Dental Floss, Yarn, Needles and Thread, Other Stringy Stuff
Puppies snuffling about at ground level will find and ingest the tiniest of objects and will end up in surgery. Most vets can tell you stories about the stuff they've surgically removed from puppies' guts.

Toilet Bowl Cleaners
If you have them, throw them out now. All dogs are born with "toilet sonar" and quickly discover that the water there is always cold.

Garage
Beware of antifreeze! It is extremely toxic and even a few drops will kill an adult Boston Terrier, less for a pup. Lock it and all other chemicals well out of reach. Fertilizers and mulch can also be toxic to dogs.

Socks and Underwear, Shoes and Slippers, Too
Keep them off the floor and close your closet doors. Puppies love all of these because they smell like you times ten!

Another consideration before bringing your puppy into the house is the safety of the dog's environment, both indoors and out. You should be aware that a small puppy can be like a toddler and that there are dangers in the household that must be eliminated.

Electrical wires should be raised off the floor and hidden from view, as they are very tempting as chewable objects. Remove breakable objects from your tables, raise cleaning supplies above the Boston's eye level and fasten garbage containers and cabinets so that puppy paws can't investigate inside them. Use barriers, such as a baby or child gate, to keep the puppy confined to a room or two (ideally the rooms with easily cleanable surfaces). A swimming pool, if you have one, can be very dangerous, so make certain that your puppy can't get into, or fall into, the pool. Some barricades will be necessary to prevent an accident. Not all dogs can swim or will be able to climb out of the pool. Watch your deck railings and make sure that your puppy cannot slip through the openings and fall.

If you are driving some distance to pick up your new Boston Terrier, take along a towel or two, a water bowl and your leash and collar. Also take along some plastic baggies and a roll of paper towels in case there are any potty accidents. You also should take someone along to help you on the journey, especially if there's a distance to drive. Your passenger will be able to hold the puppy on his lap (on a towel, of course). If no one is available to help, it may be time to introduce the puppy to his crate. Soon enough, he'll lie down and take a nap.

If you have young children in the house, you must see that they understand that the small puppy is a living being and must be treated gently. They cannot pull his ears, pick him up and drop him, carelessly sit

upon him or otherwise handle the puppy roughly. This is your responsibility! A child taught about animals at an early age can become a lifelong compassionate animal lover and

If the breeder has children in his family, the pups will already be accustomed to young people before they go to new homes.

owner. Use your common sense in all of these things. Consider where a young child can get into trouble and your puppy will be right there!

When your pup comes into the house for the first time (after he has relieved himself outside), let him look at his new home and surroundings, and give him a light meal and some water. When he is tired, take him outside again and then tuck him into his crate, either to take a nap or, hopefully, to sleep through the night.

The first day or two for your puppy should be fairly quiet. He will then have time to get used to his new home, surroundings and family members. The first night he may cry a bit, but if you put one of his new safe chew toys in his crate, this will give him some comfort and company. A radio playing soft music or a television set can also be helpful; if it doesn't comfort the puppy, at least it will drown out the whining so you can get to sleep. Seriously, don't let the puppy's whining force you to run to him. Remember, he has been uprooted from a sibling or two, his mother, and his familiar breeder, and he will need a day or two to get used

to his new family. After he finishes his fussing, he'll go to sleep. If you run to the puppy to comfort him every time he makes a peep, you'll teach him that he can control you. You are the top dog, the one in charge of bedtime. If he should cry during the first night, let him be and he will eventually quiet down and sleep. By the third night, he should be well settled in. Have patience and, within a week or less, it will seem to you, your family and the puppy that you have all been together for years.

You are now off to an excellent start with your puppy. As the days go by, you will quickly find more items that you will need, including more chew toys, a nice doggy bed for the family room and a retractable leash for walks in the park. You will need grooming supplies and a good pooper-scooper for the yard. These items can be acquired as needed from your local pet-supply shop.

SOCIAL BUTTERFLY

It's time to get your Boston out about town, or at least the neighborhood. Socializing your puppy is vital to the upbringing of a well-behaved, likeable Boston that will fit into your home and life. What a pleasure to own a dog that is a good companion and is enjoyed by everyone! Socializing begins the minute you pick your puppy up and cradle him in your arms. He knows he's special—he knows he's loved.

Introduce the puppy to the whole family, one person at a time. Hold off on the welcome-puppy party. Keep the affair civilized and orderly. Dogs like order, especially proper Bostons. The puppy will spend time meeting each family member and maybe even the family cat. Don't hurry the introductions. Let the puppy set the pace.

Once the pup's inoculations are complete, you can expand his horizons beyond the living room and back yard.

It's time to meet the neighborhood. Many lessons converge here. The puppy must learn to wear his collar, walk on a lead, behave properly when he meets strangers and other dogs and ride in the car like a

How the pup reacts to certain types of handling tells much about his temperament. Does he fidget when his feet are touched? Is he comfortable in a belly-up (submissive) position?

gentleman. This is all a part of his proper Boston education. He's on his way toward becoming a good canine citizen.

Riding in the car means that he must learn good manners in the car. You should get your Boston Terrier used to riding in the car at an early age. Most dogs love to go for rides and, if given the opportunity, they would gladly take the wheel! The safest way for your dog to travel in the car is in his crate or a travel carrier. Or you may partition the back of a larger vehicle with a special metal gate or even use a doggie seat belt. You want to keep him from running about, as he could be injured if the quickly in any kind of warm weather, especially in summer, and the dog will not be able to cope with the heat. Bostons overheat quickly. Further, leaving a window cracked could attract a dog thief or incite the dog to try to escape.

Your family might be tempted to haul the whole lot of them home, but it's probably best to start off with just one!

car stops short or he could distract the driver.

It is very important to remember not to take your dog out on a hot day and leave him alone for even a few minutes in the car. A car can heat up very

NAMING YOUR PUPPY

The first question people will ask you will be "What's your Boston's name?" You should decide this within the first day or two of his arrival.

Sometimes it may take a week

or so before you find a name that fits the dog. Other times you will have him named before you bring the puppy into the house. In general, short one- or two-syllable names are the easiest for training. Some famous Boston names from the past include: Gidget, Boots, Mamie, Mitzie, Ace, Dempsey, Simon and Belle. Choose a name that fits your pup's personality and one that you feel suits a Boston like yours best.

Let the children and other people you meet call the puppy by name as they pet him. Praise little Gidget for sitting still for the petting. Give her a treat after the company leaves, or you can allow a well-behaved child to offer the puppy a treat. You want your Boston to think that meeting people is fun and that everyone in town smells like liver treats!

WELCOMING THE BOSTON TERRIER

Overview

- Along with bowls, collar and leash, ID tag, food and toys, your most important puppy purchase for training and safety is a sturdy crate.
- You must puppy-proof your home and remove all dangers that can cause a puppy harm.
- All members of the family should be prepared, especially children who should have been taught how to properly treat their new puppy.
- Give your pup a low-key homecoming so that he's not overwhelmed by the change.
- Socialize your pup by introducing him to new people and places. Encourage people to use his name and make all new experiences positive ones.

Feeding Your Boston Terrier

Feeding and nutrition for your puppy have never been easier, thanks to the many scientifically advanced pet food companies. These food companies hire many scientists and spend millions of dollars on research to determine what will be a healthy diet for your dog. Your breeder should have been feeding a premium puppy food, and you should continue with the same brand. As the dog matures, you will change over to the adult formula, likely of the same brand. Do not add vitamins or anything else unless your veterinarian suggests that you do so. Do not think by cooking up a special

Gather 'round! Breeders often use circular bowls like this to allow the entire litter to eat together.

diet that you will turn out a product that will be more nutritious than what the dog food companies are providing.

PUPPY MEALS

Since Boston Terrier puppies are often 10 or 12 weeks old by the time they are placed in pet homes, your puppy will eat three meals a day until he's 12 weeks old. Once he's 12 weeks of age, you can divide his portion into two meals a day, morning and night (skipping the lunch serving). In the middle of the day, you can offer him a crunchy dog biscuit for a little fun, good chewing and nutrients. If you plan to switch from the food fed by your breeder, take home a small supply of the breeder's food to mix with your own to aid your puppy's adjustment to his new food. Gradually increase the ratio of new food to old until his meals consist entirely of the new food.

Digging in! A typical Boston will approach mealtime with vigor and enthusiasm.

Your Boston Terrier will not need very large bowls, but he will need sturdy, chew-resistant bowls that are easy to keep clean.

Most breeders suggest two meals a day for the life of the dog. Free feeding, that is, leaving a bowl of food available all day, is not recommended and can foster picky eating habits. Free feeders are also more likely to become possessive of their food bowls, a problem behavior that signals the beginning of aggression. Scheduled meals also give you one more opportunity to remind your Boston that all good things in life come from you—his owner and chef.

With scheduled meals, it's easier to predict elimination, which is the better road to house-training. Regular meals also help you know just how much your puppy eats and when, which is valuable information for weight control and if your pup or dog gets sick.

Always have fresh drinking water available. This may include a bowl of water in the kitchen and another in the yard for time spent outdoors. At night, you will want to take away the puppy's water bowl around 7 o'clock. This will assist in the house-training process. If he gets thirsty, give him an ice cube to lick; he'll love it!

ADULT DIETS

By the time your Boston Terrier reaches eight months of age, you will be changing over to an adult-formula dog food. Your Boston Terrier should have a premium-quality food to provide the proper balance of the vitamins, minerals and fatty acids that are necessary to support healthy bone, muscle, skin and coat. The major dog-food manufacturers have developed their formulas with strict controls, using only quality ingredients obtained from reliable sources. The labels on the food bags tell you what products are in the food (beef, chicken, corn, etc.), and list ingredients in descending order of weight or

A good diet gives your Boston energy to run and play, although he should be allowed to rest for a while before and after mealtimes to promote healthy digestion. Exercise too close to feeding time is not good for dogs.

amount in the food. You can check your dog-food bag for the amount, per pound of weight, that you should be feeding your dog daily.

To the dry kibble, you may add water to moisten and possibly a tablespoon or so of a canned brand of dog food for flavor. Keep a good covering of flesh over his ribs, but do not let your "Roundhead" become too round elsewhere! On occasion, you can add a little broth or cooked beef or chicken to your adult Boston's bowl, but it's not necessary for his balanced diet, just as a

Just like a balanced diet, fresh water is an essential part of your Boston's good health.

special treat now and then.

Avoid giving table scraps, but you can give healthy dog treats—just don't overdo it. Do not add your own supplements, "people food" or extra vitamins to the food. You will only upset the nutritional balance of the food, which could lead to obesity or fussy eating habits. Further, some "people foods" (including chocolate, onions, nuts, grapes and raisins) are toxic to dogs.

FEEDING FOR FITNESS
Like people, puppies and adult dogs have different appetites; some will lick their food bowls clean and beg for more, while others pick at their food and leave some of it untouched. It's easy to overfeed a chow hound. Who can resist those pleading Boston eyes? Be strong and stick to the meal plan! Chubby puppies may be cute and cuddly, but the extra weight is not good for a developing puppy. Overweight pups also

tend to grow into overweight adults who tire easily and will be more susceptible to other health problems. Consult your breeder and your vet for advice on how to adjust meal portions as your puppy grows.

How do you know if you're overfeeding your Boston? To check your Boston's figure, you should be able to see a "waistline" when viewing your dog from above and see a "tuck-up" in his abdominal area when viewing him from the side. If your adult Boston is overweight, you can switch to a "light" food, which has fewer calories and more fiber. "Senior" foods for older dogs have formulas designed to meet the needs of less active older dogs. Finally, consider that what and how much you feed your Boston is a major factor in his overall health and longevity. It's worth your investment in extra time and dollars to provide the best diet for your dog.

FEEDING YOUR BOSTON TERRIER
Overview

- A complete and balanced dog food is the easiest way to ensure that your Boston is getting the nutrition that he needs at each stage of life.
- The frequency of your puppy's feedings will be reduced as he grows, and eventually he will be switched to an adult dog-food formula.
- Scheduled meals, rather than free feeding, is beneficial for your dog in many aspects.
- A good adult food, fed in proper portions, should maintain your Boston in good condition for most of his life.
- Avoid table scraps, use treats wisely and make sure that your Boston stays at a healthy weight.

CHAPTER 8

House-Training Your Boston Terrier

Grass is the preferred potty spot for most dogs. Whether in your yard or on the curbside, always clean up after your Boston.

A dog's life needs structure, and your Boston Terrier will do best if his life is kept on a schedule. Dogs are creatures of habit: they like to wake, eat, play, go for walks, sleep and so forth in the same pattern every day. When your pup first comes home, do not play with him constantly, as he is very young and needs time to rest up and sleep. Keep him to a schedule as much as you can so that he will learn the routine very quickly. If he knows that you rise at 7:00 every morning, and shortly after that you will take him out, he will learn to wait for you to let him out rather than relieving himself in his crate.

Habits, both good and bad ones, that are learned at an early age become lifelong habits, so it is best to start out on the right foot. For example, don't allow your Boston to chew on the legs of your old patio furniture and think that it's cute; before long, he will be gnawing on the feet of your expensive dining-room table. Set limits and make sure that the pup sticks to them.

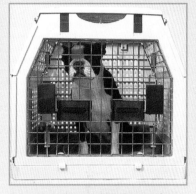

An enclosed crate like this is often used for a travel crate. Inside the home, a wire crate will be more appreciated by your pup, who will like to see all that's going on around him.

These same principles apply to the pup's toilet routine. Good habits translate to clean habits, and hence the beginning of house-training. Bostons are bright dogs and learn the house rules practically automatically. Keep the pup confined to a specific area, such as the kitchen and family room, until he is trained and fairly mature. Use baby gates and he will quickly learn that he is welcome in certain areas of the house and not welcome in other areas. And, of

Litters are often raised on newspaper, which is why paper inside the crate is a no-no. He already associates the paper with potty, and you don't want him to think it's OK to soil his crate.

course, put him in his crate when you go out so that he learns to be comfortable in his "house" and he will sleep until you return.

The house-training process should begin as soon as you bring puppy home. Do not think that you can delay this job just because you have a small dog! Diligence during the first two or three weeks will surely pay off many times over the life of the dog. Luckily, this should be a relatively easy job, since the Boston is not only smart but also tidy and well dressed.

Every time your puppy wakes up from a nap, he

The crate has very many benefits in training your Boston Terrier and keeping him safe. Besides providing him with a secure place of his own in the home, it is an invaluable tool for house-training, travel safety and having a place for him to go when you cannot supervise.

should be quickly taken outside. Watch him and praise him—"Good boy!"—when he urinates or defecates. Give him a pat on the head and bring him back inside. He may have a few accidents but, with the appropriate "No" from you, he will quickly learn that it is better to go outside and do his business than to do it on the kitchen floor and be scolded. If you catch him in the act, shout "No," pick him up, quickly put his leash on and whisk him to his outside potty area. The key here is *in the act*. If you notice a puddle or pile even one minute after it happens, you are too late. The pup won't make the connection and will think he is being scolded for no reason.

You will soon learn the habits of your dog. However, at the following times it is essential to take your dog out: when he gets up in the morning, after he eats, before he goes to bed and after long naps. Pups will require more frequent trips, but most adult dogs will only have to go out three or four times a day. Some dogs will go to the door and bark when they want to be let out, and others will nervously circle around. Watch and learn from your dog's signs.

Of course, crates are a major help in house-training, as most dogs will not want to dirty their living quarters. Introduce the crate as soon as he comes home so he learns that this is his own special bedroom. This is best accomplished with some tasty treats. For the first day or two, toss a tiny treat into the crate to entice him to go in. Pick a crate command, such as "Kennel," "Inside" or "Crate," and use it every time he enters.

Your puppy should sleep in his crate from his very first night—do not allow the puppy to sleep in your bed with you. One of your reasons for buying a dog should not be to have a warm furry body to sleep next to. To a dog, on the bed means equal, which is not a good idea this early on as you are trying to establish your leadership.

Don't spoil your Boston. Even if he whines at first and objects to the confinement, be firm and stay the course. If you release him when he cries, you provide his first life lesson…if I cry, I get to go to bed with mommy (here's a lesson in parenting, too).

A better scheme is to place the crate next to your bed at night for the first few weeks. Your presence will comfort him, and you'll also know if he needs a midnight potty trip. Make a practice of placing your puppy in his crate for naps, at nighttime and whenever you are unable to watch him closely. Not to worry…he will let you know when he wakes up and needs a potty trip. If he falls asleep under the table, guess what he'll do first when he wakes up? Make a puddle, then toddle over to say "Hi!"

Despite its many benefits, crate use can be abused. The crate is not a prison. You cannot use it to punish the puppy one minute and then cheerfully announce "Crate time" and expect the puppy to willingly run over to the Puppy Penitentiary. Keep the association with the crate happy, positive and fun. Also, do not overuse the crate. Puppies under 12 weeks of age should never be confined for more than two hours at a time, unless, of course, they are sleeping. A general rule of thumb is three hours maximum for a three-month old pup, four to five hours for the four- to five-month-old, and no more than six hours for dogs over six months of age. If you're unable to be home to release the dog, arrange for a relative, neighbor or dog-sitter to let him out to exercise and potty.

Some Boston owners prefer to paper-train their dogs, even though crates are still used to a lesser extent. If you prefer to paper-train your Boston puppy, the routine is basically the same. Assign an out-of-the-way elimination place (in front of the back door?) and cover it with newspaper. Take your puppy to the designated papered area on schedule. Use the specified potty word, and praise when he does his business. Do not use the area for any other purpose except potty breaks. Keep the area clean. You can place a small piece of soiled paper on the clean ones to remind puppy why he's there. His nose will tell him what to do.

Even if you paper-train, you will use the crate to confine the puppy when you're out of the house. If not, what can you do with your uncrated puppy when you're not home? How sure can you be that he's not getting himself into danger, destroying your belongings or otherwise creating havoc in your house? If you are crate-shy (and some people are), then you can confine him to one room with baby gates or another dog-proof barrier. Puppy-proof the room by removing anything pup could chew or damage and hurt himself in the process. But even in a stripped environment, some pups will chew through drywall. An exercise pen, 4 feet by 4 feet square (available through pet suppliers), sturdy enough that pup can't knock it down, will provide safe containment for short periods. Paper one area for elimination, with perhaps a blanket in the opposite corner for napping. Safe chew toys should help keep him happy and occupied while you're gone.

As with other aspects of dog training, you must be patient. House-training, especially, can be a trying time. It is simply essential to have a clean house dog, and life will be much easier for all of you—not to mention the carpeting and furniture. Keep in mind while training: use your common sense, be consistent and have patience. Just when you may think that all is hopeless, your puppy turns into the perfect little American gentleman.

HOUSE-TRAINING YOUR BOSTON TERRIER

Overview

- In all you do with your puppy, house-training especially, structure and consistency are essential to success.
- Use your crate and baby gates to confine your puppy to certain rooms before he is fully house-trained.
- A puppy will require many potty trips each day. Be sure to praise him when he "goes" and do not scold him unless you catch him in the act.
- Use your crate correctly; do not abuse it! When used properly, it is a wonderful tool and your Boston will love it.
- Whether or not you crate-train, you still must ensure your pup's safety when you are not home or cannot supervise.

Grooming Your Boston Terrier

Your Boston Terrier wakes up every morning in his dapper tuxedo, but you have to make sure it's neat, tidy and shiny clean. That black and white outer coat, fortunately, is quite easy to maintain, being a short coat that doesn't require any special care other than regular brushing. A big plus with the Boston Terrier is that there is a very minimal amount of grooming required: no stripping knives, fancy electric clippers, special dryers or curlers involved.

Just because it's so simple, don't

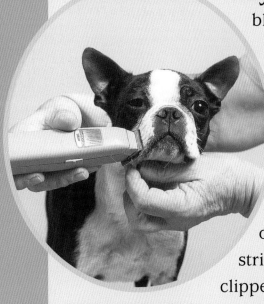

Owners may sometimes trim whiskers for a neat appearance, but this is completely optional.

forget that you still have to do it at least once a week. Brushing with a soft- to medium-bristle brush is recommended to keep your dog's coat looking his best. Your local pet-supply shop should offer an ample selection of brushes and other grooming devices. Buy a top-quality bristle brush and it will last for the life of your dog. Another "handy" device is the grooming mitt—it fits over your hand, with soft wire pins on one side and smooth fabric on the other. These are made with coats like the Boston Terrier's smooth, sleek one in mind.

In addition to brushing, you may want to go over your Boston's coat with a comb, with the teeth spaced close together.

Although Bostons aren't difficult to bathe, given their small size and amiable dispositions, it's not necessary to bathe them more than a few times a year. Show dogs, however, could be bathed before every show. The white on the Boston's tux should be white-white! For pet Bostons, additional baths are

Large eyes, like those of the Boston, are more prone to getting scratched or to getting dirt and debris inside. Check your Boston's eyes frequently and keep the eye areas clean.

CHAPTER 9

needed only if they decide to explore the terrier side of their name (which is to say, when they've muddied their paws in *terra firma*). Under normal circumstances, for everyday dust and dirt, a rubdown with a damp cloth will be ample for

Your young pup can be cradled on your lap for his pedicures, making sure he holds still.

cleaning. Frequent bathing deprives the dog's coat of important oils, so it's best to bathe the dog only two or three times a year unless otherwise needed. Make a bath part of your dog's change

of season! Speaking of seasons, if you have an unspayed bitch, you will want to give her a good bath (or two) after her heat cycle. This helps to keep your house clean and the neighbors' dogs farther away.

It is important to trim your Boston's toenails, and it is best to start this within a week of bringing him home. Purchase a quality toenail trimmer for dogs. You may want to purchase a styptic stick in case you trim the nail too short and bleeding starts. If your dog's toenails are light in color, you will easily see the blood vessel that runs inside the nail. However, it is a bit more difficult to see it in dark-nailed dogs, and you may nick the blood vessel until you are more familiar with trimming the nails. If you do not start trimming the nails at a young age, so that your dog becomes used to the procedure, you will have greater difficulty in trimming the nails as the dog becomes older and more resistant. If your Boston doesn't like the feeling of the guillotine-style clipper, which is recommended for small dogs, you can purchase a battery-operated nail grinder with a sandpaper head. Some dogs don't mind this device, and there's the extra advantage of not nicking the dog's blood vessel.

This handsome chap's natural beauty requires very little of his doting owner. A weekly once-over with a bristle brush or glove and

trimming the toenails, along with regular toothbrushing and checking his ears, eyes and anal glands for problems, are all that are required to keep your Boston Terrier looking his black-tie best.

Your Boston's upright ears make it easy for you to look inside and check for problems. Healthy ears should be cleaned weekly.

GROOMING YOUR BOSTON TERRIER

Overview

- The Boston is a naturally dapper gentleman in his tuxedo. He does not require fancy grooming, only routine attention, to look his best.
- A good-quality bristle brush and a grooming mitt are good tools for grooming your Boston's sleek coat.
- Too-frequent bathing is not good for a dog's coat and skin. For a pet Boston, bathe him only a few times yearly unless otherwise needed.
- Nail trimming, toothbrushing and regular checks of the eyes, ears and anal glands are "housekeeping" tasks that should be part of your grooming routine for good health.

Your Boston Terrier in Good Health

I n addition to being a well-informed, respon-sible owner, you also need a good veterinarian to sustain your Boston Terrier in good health. Finding a veteri-narian can pose considerable difficulty for some owners, depending on where they live. In some rural areas, owners encounter vets who mainly know farm animals or horses. It's important that you find a vet who knows small dogs or at least dogs in general. In suburban and

At your pup's first visit, the vet will decide how to proceed with the vacci-nation schedule.

urban areas, you should have little difficulty, and you likely will have your pick of a few different clinics. Your breeder, if from your area, should be able to recommend someone; otherwise, it will be your job to find a clinic that you like.

A big consideration in finding a veterinarian is to find someone, for convenience, who is within ten miles of your home. Find a veterinarian you like and trust and in whom you feel confident that he knows what he is doing. See that the office looks and smells clean. It is your right to check on fees before setting up an appointment. If you have a satis-factory visit, take the business card so that you have the clinic's number and the name of the veterinarian that you saw. Try and see the same veteri-narian at each visit, as he will personally know the history of your dog and your dog will be familiar with him. At the very least, your

Healthy teeth are a major part of your Boston's overall health, as dental problems can lead to serious problems with the internal organs.

Boston Terriers can be affected by skin problems caused by pollen and grass allergies.

healthy Boston should visit the vet annually for a full check-up, booster shots if needed, heartworm preventive and overall assessment. For older dogs, twice yearly is suggested to catch any problems early on.

Inquire whether the clinic takes emergency calls; if they do not, as many no longer do, get the name, address and telephone number of the emergency veterinary service in your area and keep this handy with your veterinarian's phone number.

VACCINES

The vaccines recommended by the American Veterinary Medical Association are called core vaccines, those which protect against diseases most dangerous to your puppy and adult dog. The first of the diseases, distemper (canine distemper virus—CDV), which at one time was the scourge of dog breeding, can be fatal in puppies, but with the proper immunization and a clean puppy-rearing area, it no longer presents a problem to the reputable breeder. Other core vaccines protect against the following diseases, all of which are highly contagious and fatal in puppies up to 16 weeks of age: canine parvovirus (CPV or parvo), canine adenovirus (CAV-2) and canine hepatitis (CAV-1). Parvovirus is recognized by fever, vomiting and diarrhea. This is a deadly disease for pups and can spread very easily through their feces. All of these disease vaccines are generally combined into what is often called a 5-way shot. On your first visit, take along the card that your breeder gave you with a record of the shots that your puppy has had so that the veterinarian will know which series of shots your pup should be getting. You should also take in a fecal sample for a worm test.

Thanks to strict rabies

laws, there is very little problem with rabid dogs and cats in our communities. Back in the 1940s, there were as many as 7,000 annual rabies cases in the US; currently, there are only about 100 cases reported annually. Owners must recognize the importance of the rabies vaccination for their dogs, understanding that an unvaccinated dog exposed to a wild animal bite could easily contract the fatal disease. In most cases, such a dog would be euthanized (or quarantined for six months). Rabies vaccinations are required by law in all 50 states, though the age at which the dog must be inoculated varies from state to state. Three to four months of age is the usual age, though owners should be familiar with the laws of their own state. In fact, some states' laws vary among different counties or towns. Once you know the laws in your state and town, discuss a rabies

vaccination plan with your vet. If possible, you might opt for the three-year shot instead of the annual shot. The recommended course would be to vaccinate every third year after the first rabies booster (given one year after the puppy series). However, some areas do require annual revaccination.

Non-core vaccines no longer routinely recommended by the AVMA, except when the risk is present, are canine parainfluenza, leptospirosis, canine corona-virus, *Bordetella* (kennel cough) and Lyme disease

There's only one way to take a dog's temperature! This is something that every dog owner should learn to do at home.

(borreliosis). Leptospirosis is an uncommon disease that affects the kidneys; it is rare in young puppies, occurring primarily in adult dogs. Your veterinarian will alert you if there is a risk of these non-fatal diseases in your town or neighborhood so you can immunize your dog accordingly.

The American Animal Hospital Association (AAHA) guidelines issued in 2003 recommend vaccinating adult dogs every three years instead of annually. Research suggests that annual vaccinations may actually be over-vaccinating and may be responsible for many of today's canine health problems. Mindful of that, the revised AAHA guidelines on vaccinations also strongly suggest that veterinarians and owners consider a dog's individual needs and exposure before they decide on a vaccine protocol. Many dog owners now do annual titer tests to check their dogs' antibodies rather than automatically vaccinating for parvo or distemper.

HEALTH CONCERNS IN BOSTONS

The Boston Terrier is, overall, a very healthy dog, but there are some problems within the breed that you should be aware of. Your breeder should be able to tell you about the occurrence of these problems in his line. Reputable breeders are willing to discuss health concerns openly with potential clients. Do not believe a breeder who has not encountered a single problem

Hot weather can pose problems for the short-faced Boston. He needs access to water, shade and, best of all, indoor air conditioning, when temperatures are high.

A shiny coat, bright eyes and alert demeanor all point toward good health internally.

in his line. He either is lying or hasn't bred more than one litter in his career.

Patellar luxation, dislocation of the kneecap, is a skeletal disorder, and reputable breeders are doing their best to eliminate it by not breeding from affected dogs. If you are taking in a rescue dog, you will want to know if your dog has this problem, as a Boston may have been given up by an owner who did not want to pay for surgery to correct it. You must take on the responsibility in such a case.

Dermatitis due to allergies is not uncommon in the Boston. Nearly 18%, in a health survey done in 2000 by the Boston Terrier Club of America, had allergy dermatitis. If your dog should start to scratch certain areas of his body, or lick his feet, you should take him to the veterinarian for a diagnosis of the problem and for proper medication or shampoos.

There are various causes for itching and excessive licking in Bostons, from inhalant, grass and food allergies to reactions to medications, neuroses and parasites.

Juvenile cataracts can also be a problem for the Boston Terrier, and you should ask your breeder if he has had the eyes of his dogs checked for any problems. A cataract is an opacity that covers the lens of the eye and will cause impairment of vision. Some cataracts affect senior dogs and may or may not lead to blindness. Veterinary science has made terrific advances in cataract surgeries, and removal of the cataracts to restore vision is a common though expensive procedure. It's better to purchase a puppy from a breeder who has screened his line for hereditary eye diseases.

The Boston Terrier is a brachycephalic breed of dog. Others include the French Bulldog, Boxer, Bulldog and any breed that has a "flat face." Because of the flat face and pushed-in nose, all of these breeds can have difficulty breathing, especially during hot weather. Care must be taken not to let the dog get overheated in the summer. Take precautions to ward off potential problems. If you live in a hot, humid area, buy an air conditioner to keep your Boston comfortable during the "dog days of summer."

When purchasing a puppy from a breeder, health guarantees are an important consideration. A responsible breeder will give you a contract that will guarantee your pup against certain congenital defects. Usually this guarantee will be limited in time to six months or one year. If there is a problem, the breeder will possibly replace the pup or offer some refund in the price. Such a guarantee assures you that the breeder stands behind his breeding program and the health of his dogs.

YOUR BOSTON TERRIER IN GOOD HEALTH

Overview

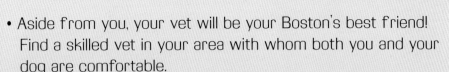

- Aside from you, your vet will be your Boston's best friend! Find a skilled vet in your area with whom both you and your dog are comfortable.
- Vaccines are no longer "one shot fits all." Discuss with your vet the proper course of inoculation for your Boston based on risk of disease, your individual dog and local laws.
- Some breed-specific health concerns include patellar luxation, dermatitis, cataracts and breathing difficulties.
- A good breeder will include a health guarantee in his sales contract.

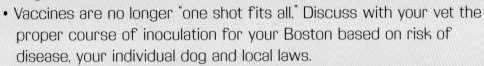

Boston Terrier University

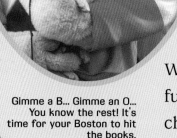

Gimme a B... Gimme an O... You know the rest! It's time for your Boston to hit the books.

The advantages of a good solid education in our modern world cannot be challenged. In order for your Boston Terrier to become an upright canine citizen, or perhaps an AKC Canine Good Citizen®, he needs a proper education.

Certainly for a Boston Terrier to be competitive in today's "dog-eat-dog" world, he will need a leg up. Get him started early. A well-socialized puppy will get along famously with his human professors and his canine fraternity or sorority mates. Welcome to Boston Terrier U! Thankfully, the puppy version is much cheaper than four years at an Ivy

League college. You won't even need to take out a loan!

SOCIALIZATION 101

Your puppy's socialization sessions are a combination of social studies and recess; in other words, just fun! The breeder began the puppy's social-ization while he was still at the breeder's home. Introducing the puppies to visiting buyers and their children encourages puppies to accept human handling. So by the time you bring your puppy home, he should be well on the road to becoming the class busybody. Since most breeders raise their Boston pups in their homes (rather than in a kennel environment), your young pupil will be used to family, strangers and the everyday noises of the home. As such, sounds like the coffee maker, shower, vacuum and telephone will not startle him.

A typical, well-socialized Boston Terrier should act as friendly as he looks.

The Boston is a naturally curious canine who enjoys socializing and exploring.

When pup comes home with you, you continue his socialization classes.

Once he's completed his inoculations, let him meet the neighbors and play for a few minutes. Take him for short walks in the park or bring him for a visit to a store where he can meet other puppies on their first leashes and their owners. Friendly environments are the key—find places where he will see nice dog people and dogs as well as hear noises he doesn't hear in your kitchen or back yard. Watch other dogs, however, as they are not always friendly. Keep your pup on a short leash and you will have control over him so he does not jump up on children or other puppies.

PKC 102

That's Puppy Kindergarten Class! Dog owners invariably realize that it's to their advantage to have obedient dogs who obey the basic commands. This investment in time and sometimes money pays off generously, as living with a reliably trained, mannerly dog is much easier than living with a four-legged monster that insists on running the household his way and disregards everything you say. Your friends and other visitors will appreciate your dog's good behavior, too.

You or one of the family members should attend Puppy Kindergarten Classes with your Boston Terrier. In most schools, puppies from two to five months of age can enroll, and it will take about two months to complete the class. Although class size varies, most have no more than a dozen canine students and their owners at a time. Any more than 12 pups at a time and you might as well be practicing at the dog park! The instructor will cover the basics: sit, heel, down and recall (or come). There are definite advantages to your puppy's learning each of these exercises. Sit and heel are great helps when walking your dog. What could be nicer than having your handsome Boston Terrier walking like a gentleman or lady at your left side and sitting as you wait to cross the street? Recall is very important if your dog escapes from the yard, slips out of his

written the following exercises are presented, it's much easier to follow an instructor in a class. You will learn by watching the instructor and from your successes and mistakes (as well as those of the other owners). Likewise,

A Boston brigade on their best behavior! Socialization and puppy classes help you mold a dog that acts politely around people and other dogs.

collar or otherwise gets away from you and you need to call him back. At moments like this, obedience has no price: it is invaluable to your dog's safety.

PKC proves helpful especially to first-time owners, as no matter how clearly

dogs learn by watching, too. Your Boston Terrier will imitate what the other puppies are doing—both good and bad. Just like raising kids, always know who your Boston is hanging out with! Ill-behaved puppies will pass their bad habits along to your dog.

Luckily, you don't have to worry about your adolescent Boston smoking or getting involved in a bad pack.

MANNERS 201

Good manners start at home. Before you enroll your Boston in an obedience school to learn the basic commands, there are certain basic behaviors he should learn. Beyond recognizing his name, your Boston Terrier should recognize and respond to the following.

Off

This is an important word for a dog as bouncy as the Boston. In no time, he will become active enough to finish off the candy dish on the coffee table (and you know what sugar does to kids—it's worse with dogs!). "Off, Tiny" and then push him down on his four feet. Again, dogs are smart, particularly Bostons, and your pup will quickly learn what "Off" means. If you do not

want him on your sofa, now is the time to teach him that. Be consistent and make sure every member of the household knows the rules. Tiny won't know what's expected of him if he's allowed to watch cartoons on the couch with the kids, but gets relegated to the floor later when dad is watching his shows.

Kennel Up

Hearing two simple words lets the dog know to go to his crate. Along with "Kennel up" you will teach "Bedtime," which also tells him to go to his crate. These two commands mean different things, so do not confuse the two. The dog will quickly learn that "Bedtime" means a treat and to bed for the night, while "Kennel up" means that you will be back in a few hours.

No

Of course, the most basic of commands, which is learned

very quickly, is "No." An extra-mischievous pup may even begin to think that his name is "No!" Say it firmly and with conviction, just once. Again, your dog will learn that this means to keep off, don't do it or don't even think about it. Just as with all of your commands, you must be firm in speaking the command "No." After the dog stops the undesirable behavior and does what you want, give him a pat on the head and praise, "Good boy." If he has achieved some great success, give him a treat along with the praise.

OK

No matter what you are doing with your Boston Terrier, you will need a word to signal that the task or exercise is over, similar to "At ease" in the military. "All done" and "Free" are also commonly recommended, but "OK" is the first choice for a release command. Whether you have just completed a lesson or just finished clipping his toenails, the "OK" indicates that he can relax and/or move from a stationary position.

Take It and Leave It

These commands offer many advantages for good manners and safety. Place a treat in

Socialization at such a tender age helps foster the dog/human bond that instills in the dog the desire to please his owner.

the palm of your hand and tell your puppy to "Take it" as he grabs the treat. Repeat three times. On the fourth time, do not say a word as your dog reaches for the treat…just close your fingers around the treat and wait. Do not pull away, but be prepared for the pup to paw, lick, bark and nibble on your fingers. Patience! When he finally pulls away from your hand and waits for a few seconds, open your hand and tell him to "Take it." Repeat until he pauses and waits for your command to "Take it."

Now the next step. Show your Boston the treat in the palm of your hand and tell him to "Leave it." When he goes for the treat, close your hand and repeat "Leave it." Repeat the process until he pulls away, wait just a second, then open your hand, tell him to "Take it" and allow him to take the treat. Repeat the "Leave it" process until he waits just a few seconds, then give the treat on "Take it." Gradually extend the time you wait after your puppy "Leaves it" and before you tell him "Take it."

Now you want to teach your Boston to leave things on the ground, not just your hand (think of all the things you don't want him to pick up). With your puppy on a loose leash, position yourself in front of him and toss a treat behind you and a little to the side so he can see it, while saying "Leave it." Here begins the dance. If he goes for the treat, use your body, not your hands, to block him, moving him backwards away from it. As soon as he backs off and gives up trying to get around you, unblock the treat and tell him "Take it." Be ready to block again if he goes for it before you give permission. Repeat the process until he understands and waits for the command.

Once your Boston knows this well, practice with his food dish, telling him to "Leave it," then "Take it" after he complies (he can either sit or stand while waiting for his dish). Gradually extend the waiting period before you tell him to "Take it."

Wait

You'll love this one, especially when your Boston comes into the house with wet or muddy paws. Work on this command with a closed interior door. (It would not be wise to try this with an outside exit door.) Start to open the door as if to go through or out. When your dog tries to follow, step in front to prevent his passage. Don't use the wait command just yet. Keep blocking until he hesitates and you can open the door a little to pass through. Then say "OK" (or whichever release command you've chosen) and let him go through the door. Repeat by stepping in his path until he understands and waits for you, then start applying the word "Wait" to the behavior. Practice in different doorways, progressing to outside entrances (to safe or enclosed areas) only after he will wait reliably.

BOSTON TERRIER UNIVERSITY

Overview

- It's time for your pup's first day at school! Before beginning the basic commands with your pup, you must lay the foundation with some early puppy lessons.
- Your pup's first course is socialization, getting used to all people, other animals, new situations, different sights and sounds, etc.
- Puppy Kindergarten Classes are wonderful for both early training and socialization. They are as effective in teaching the puppy as they are in teaching you, the owner, how to teach your puppy.
- Some early commands, for both good manners and puppy's safety, include Off, No, OK, Take it/Leave it, Wait and commands to tell pup that it's crate time.

CHAPTER 12

Your Boston's Curriculum

A gentle push on the rump guides your Boston into position so that he will know what to do when you say "Sit."

Boston Terriers are fairly easy dogs to train: they are smart and attentive, and they like doing things. Don't forget that the Boston is a little guy (or gal), and you cannot be forceful or rough when training him. You have to treat him gently and with care, and he will soon trust you and obey you. As long as you have the time and patience, you will be successful with your dog. It's important that you assume the role of instructor, professor and "know-it-all." You have to convince your bright little Boston student that you know what you're doing (even if this is your first time training a dog). Never let your Boston undergrad see you sweat! Also, be certain that you are introducing and executing your lessons the same way every time. Don't say "Sit" today and "Sit down" tomorrow. Don't use a treat lure on Monday and then just push on his rear quarters to make him sit on Tuesday. Consistency applies to the teacher and the student.

Your Boston must be used to wearing his collar and leash before training can begin.

One common problem encountered by trainers is anticipation. The dog learns by repetition, but you cannot practice a command 37 times in a row. Three or four times, and move on to another exercise. Once the dog learns the sit, stay and down positions, you must mix them up so that he cannot anticipate your next command. Many dogs will sit and give you their paw as soon as they see a treat. Backpedaling to correct something learned incorrectly is much more difficult

Teaching the dog to stay in a standing position is a must for show dogs and can be useful for pets, too.

than establishing an effective lesson plan from the start.

THE LESSON PLAN

Now that your Boston Terrier is on his way to having some canine etiquette, let's move on to your dog's formal education. Here we discuss the basic commands that all well-trained dogs are expected to know, required for graduation from Boston Terrier U. If you attend obedience training classes, you will have professional help in learning these commands. However, with a little time and effort, you and your dog can learn these very basic exercises on your own. Remember, teach each command the same way every time, and do not lose your patience with the dog, as he will not understand what you are doing. Also, reward him for doing his command properly. Your Boston puppy should learn these commands very quickly. Let's discuss the

Your hand held with the palm facing the dog helps to reinforce the verbal "Stay" command.

sit, stay, heel, come and down exercises.

Sit

The sit is the exercise with which you should begin. Place your dog on your left side as you are standing and firmly say "Sit." As you say this, run your hand down your dog's back and gently guide him into a sitting position. Praise him, hold him in this position for a few moments, release your hand, praise him again and give him a treat. Repeat this several times a day, perhaps as many as ten times, and, before long,

your pup will understand what you want. Some Bostons will squirm a little when you touch their hindquarters, so another option is to hold a treat high above the dog's nose. As he looks up to see the treat, he will automatically sit. As he sits, say "Sit." He'll figure it out within just a few ounces of liver!

Stay

The stay command is possibly the easiest of all. Teach your dog to stay in a seated position until you call him. Have your dog sit and, as you say "Stay," place your hand in front of his nose and take a step or two away. Don't go any farther than two steps to start. After ten seconds or so, call your dog. If he gets up before the end of the command, have him sit again and repeat the stay command. When he stays until called (remembering to start with a very short period of time), praise him and give him a

treat. As he learns this command, increase the space that you move away from the dog as well as the length of time that he stays.

Heel

Now let's talk about the heel command. Have your dog on your left side, with his leash on, and teach him to walk

Heeling means that *you* set the pace of your walks, not the dog!

Once your Boston is comfortable in the down position, he will perform the exercise without your physically guiding him.

with you. If your pup lunges forward, give the leash a quick snap and say a firm "No." Then continue to walk your dog, praising him as he walks nicely by your side. Again, if he lunges, snap his leash quickly and say a smart "No." He will quickly learn that it is easier and more pleasant to walk by your side. Never allow him to lunge or jump up at someone passing by you. Heeling is helpful for show pups, too, who have to walk politely on lead as they gait for the judge.

Come

Begin to practice this vital exercise with the puppy on his leash and in a safely confined area. You can't afford to risk failure or the pup will learn he does not have to come when called. Even though Boston Terriers aren't terriers in the traditional sense, they absolutely love the prospect of chasing a squirrel, the neighbor's cat or some other enticing furry critter. "Come" has to be obeyed 110% of the time for safety's sake.

Once you have the pup's attention, happily call to him from a short distance: "Puppy, come!" When he comes to you, give him a treat (but don't touch him). If he hesitates, reel him in (that's why he's on lead). Hold his collar with one hand as you dispense the treat. The collar grasp is important. You will eventually phase out the treat and switch to hands-on praise only. This maneuver also connects holding his collar with coming and treating, which will assist you in countless future behaviors.

Do 10 or 12 repetitions, 2 or 3 times a day. Once your pup has mastered the come, continue to practice daily to imprint this most important behavior onto his brain. Remember, though, "off leash" is often synonymous with "out of control." Always keep your Boston Terrier on his leash when not in a fenced or confined area.

Down

The down will probably be the most difficult of the basic commands to teach. This position is not a natural position for dogs and requires more patience on your part and lots of trust on the part of your Boston. Begin with your Boston in the sit position; kneel down next to him and place your right hand under his front legs and your left hand on his shoulders. As you softly say "Down," gently push his front legs out into the down position. Once you have him down, talk gently to him, stroke his back so that he will be comfortable and then praise him. Many Bostons do not like learning the down command, but with practice and a gentle approach, you can succeed. Lengthen the time period that you expect your Boston to retain the position. Once he realizes that the down is not so scary, he will become used to the down position.

YOUR BOSTON'S CURRICULUM

Overview

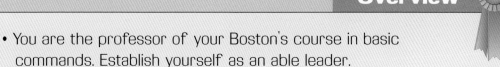

- You are the professor of your Boston's course in basic commands. Establish yourself as an able leader.
- Before you begin, formulate a lesson plan for success.
- The basic commands can be taught at home or augmented with an obedience class.
- The essentials are Sit, Stay, Heel, Come and Down. These are important for both safety and good behavior.

Home Care for Your Boston Terrier

Can you train your Boston to brush his own teeth? Not likely . . .

To give your Boston Terrier a healthy advantage in life, you must become your Boston Terrier's home healthcare aide. It's all a matter of good housekeeping so that you can qualify for the good owner's seal of approval. You also must know your Boston Terrier and recognize changes that may indicate a problem and warrant a trip to the veterinarian. The rewards are many, including a healthy, happy Boston Terrier that looks up to you for his care, affection and education.

GOOD HOUSEKEEPING

Don't forget the usual "housekeeping" with your new puppy. While your dog is a young pup, you should start getting him used to the basic examination routine. Each time you groom your Boston, you should check over his ears, eyes and teeth. Ears should be checked for dirt or any sign of infection. Take a cotton ball or damp cloth—a soft washcloth can work quite well—and gently wash the inside of the ear. If you notice any build-up of wax or a putrid smell, you should take your dog to the veterinarian to have his ears checked and cleaned. If there is an infection, the vet will prescribe an ointment or liquid to clear up the problem. Dogs with upright ears have more of a chance of dirt getting into the ears, whereas dogs with drop ears have a "warm" ear where infections can grow more easily. If you see your dog shaking his head from side to side, or

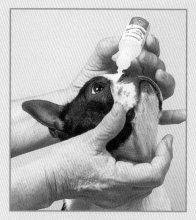

For small eye problems, the vet may prescribe eye drops.

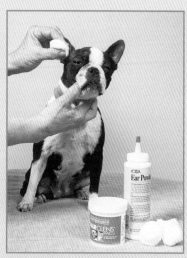

Ear cleaner and a cotton ball, or premoistened pads, make it easy to keep your Boston's ears clean.

CHAPTER 13

pushing his head and ears along the sides of the furniture or carpet, you can be almost certain that an ear infection is in the making.

When grooming, take another damp cloth and gently wash around the eyes. Dogs with folds around the eyes and nostrils can have a build-up of matter that should be wiped clean on a daily basis. All dogs should have their eyes checked if any redness appears. Quite often you can purchase an over-the-counter medication at the pet shop to clear up a small problem. If an eye problem persists, you will have to see your veterinarian.

When dealing with the Boston's teeth, it's no mere game of "tooth or dare"—you are your Boston's dentist, too! Small dogs notoriously have poor bites and weak teeth, although the Boston Terrier hasn't as many problems as the toy breeds. You still must put your dog's dental care on the top of your "to-do" list. The mouth should be checked and the teeth brushed on a regular basis. You can clean your dog's teeth yourself by using a specially made doggie tooth-brush; a frugal doggie dentist can use a piece of washcloth or a piece of gauze, wrapped around a finger. If not using the toothbrush, use the cloth or gauze as you would a tooth-brush by gently rubbing your finger back and forth across the teeth. Do not use human tooth-paste; you will find doggie toothpaste available at the pet shop. Again, for those of you who wish to save a little money, baking soda works fairly well but doesn't taste as good as the doggie pastes. Brushing the teeth also ensures that your dog's breath will be pleasant when he goes to kiss you good night.

Your Boston Terrier's teeth are worth the investment of your time (and money) because if you allow plaque to build up in your dog's mouth, you will have to deal with the cost of a veterinary tooth-cleaning or, worse, dealing with a related illness. Veterinarians will clean your dog's teeth (also called scaling), but it is a costly process and will not need to be done if you have been a diligent doggie dentist. You may purchase a dental scraper and clean the teeth yourself, though you would profit from watching the vet do the job first, as it requires more skill than the routine brushing. Another way to avoid plaque build-up is to give your Boston a couple of hard dog biscuits a day; this, in addition to his dry kibble, will keep his choppers white and strong.

As the dog ages, as in his human master, his gums may recede and he may have further problems. Your vet may tell you that it is necessary to remove one, or more, teeth, but most dogs continue to eat well even if all of their teeth have been pulled. Of course, their diet will be a bit different, but they will fare just as well. A distinctly

Home care for your Boston includes having all of the supplies that you will need.

unpleasant odor from the mouth is a signal that all is not well with your dog's gums or teeth.

Now let's go to the other end: all dogs have anal sacs located on either side of the rectum. The foul contents are used to mark the dog's territory and are usually released when the dog defecates. When the anal glands aren't working properly, they will have to be expressed by hand. Expressing the anal glands is not the most pleasant of tasks. Besides being quite smelly, it is tricky to do properly. You may find that it is easier to have this done at your Boston's annual vet visit. You can ask your veterinarian to show you how to do this the first time and then you can do it at home if you wish.

A sign that the anal glands are clogged is that your dog is scooting his bottom across the floor. This is not a new dance step, it's a sign to take care of his anal glands. On occasion, the glands may appear swollen, which can be seen on a smooth-coated dog like your Boston Terrier. Impacted glands require veterinary assistance, sometimes surgery, to clean them out.

The eyes, ears, teeth and anal glands are part of the good housekeeping of dog ownership. Start your dog on this routine at a very early age, doing a bit at a time, and,

when your dog is an adult, you will have little difficulty in performing these cleaning tasks.

A WORD ABOUT BUGS

Parasites can be a problem, and there are certain ones that you should be aware of. Heartworm can be a deadly problem; dogs in some parts of the country can be more prone to this than in others. Heartworms become very massive and wrap themselves around the heart; if not treated, the dog will eventually die. In the spring, call your veterinarian and ask if your dog should have a heartworm test. If so, take him to the clinic and he will be given a test to make certain that he is clear of heartworm; then he will be put on heartworm-preventive medication. This is important, particularly if you live in areas where mosquitoes are present.

Fleas are also a problem,

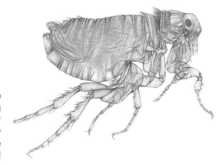

A close-up view of dog enemy number one—the flea!

but particularly in the warmer parts of the country or during warmer weather months. You can purchase flea powder or a collar from the pet shop or ask your veterinarian what he suggests that you use. Some preventives are available by prescription only. If you suspect fleas, lay your dog on his side, separate the coat to the skin and look for any skipping, jumping or skittering around of little bugs.

Ticks are more prevalent in areas where there are numerous trees. Ticks are small (to start) and dark, and they like to attach themselves to the warm parts of the ears, the leg pits, the face folds, etc. The longer they are on the dog, the bigger they become, filling themselves with your pet's blood and becoming as big as a dime. Take your forceps and carefully pull the tick out to make sure you get the pincers. Promptly plunge the tick into household bleach or light a match to it. Put alcohol on the wound and a dab of antibiotic salve. It's wise to protect your dog. Certain flea preventives are effective against ticks, too.

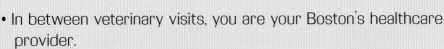

HOME CARE FOR YOUR BOSTON TERRIER

Overview

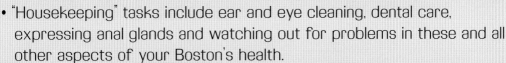

- In between veterinary visits, you are your Boston's healthcare provider.
- "Housekeeping" tasks include ear and eye cleaning, dental care, expressing anal glands and watching out for problems in these and all other aspects of your Boston's health.
- Begin routine home examinations when your Boston is a pup.
- Every owner must deal with parasite control. The vet can suggest suitable preventives for your Boston.

Keeping Your Boston Terrier Active

The Boston, in his black-tie best and striking a show pose, is quite a sight in the show ring.

B ecause your Boston Terrier is grouped as a "Non-Sporting Dog" doesn't mean that he's not a sporty, active fellow. Bostons like keeping busy and feeling useful. You may find that your Boston Terrier flies through his lessons and is always champing at the bit to learn more. If you're lucky enough to own one of these over-achievers, then take advantage of his smarts and get involved in some organized events.

Dog shows can be exciting weekend events for dog and owner. Provided that your Boston Terrier is registered with the AKC and doesn't have any disqualifying faults (including being neutered/spayed), he can enter a dog show. You both will have to practice the routine at home, setting him up on a grooming table for evaluation and gaiting him on a short lead around the yard. The basic commands, especially heel, stand and stay, will be of great assistance when working with the dog in the show ring. Although your dog may not be selected as first in his class, you will

For trips to dog shows, it helps to have your Boston accustomed to a travel crate.

have lots of fun meeting the show people, learning about the sport of conformation showing and exchanging fun Boston tales with fellow Bostonians. You'll quickly learn that "there's no people like (dog) show people," and they are an eccentric, effervescent and talkative clan with much to share.

There are many other kinds of competitive events that will challenge your Boston Terrier. Beyond dog shows, which are the most popular

With the greatest of ease! This Boston veritably flies through the agility course.

The Boston shows his red, white and blue heritage by clearing a jump while displaying the stars and stripes.

sport for Boston Terriers, you and your dog may enjoy obedience trials, agility trials, flyball, Rally-O or any other special events that you can discover together. Even though they are small, Boston Terriers can excel in many activities because of their intelligence and high energy level. To begin, after graduating from Puppy Kindergarten Classes and Boston Terrier University, you may want to work toward a Canine Good Citizen® (CGC) award. This American Kennel Club-sponsored program is geared toward well-trained companion dogs. When successfully completed, the CGC award indicates that your dog is obediently trained and will respond reliably at home, in public places and with other dogs.

The CGC program is available to dogs of any age; it's both fun and useful for everyday life. There are ten steps: accepting a friendly stranger, sitting politely for petting, accepting light grooming and examination from a stranger, walking on a loose lead, coming when called, responding calmly to another dog, responding to distractions, down on command and remaining calm when the owner is out of sight for three minutes. Upon successful completion, your Boston will receive an AKC Canine Good Citizen® certificate and the CGC suffix to add to your Boston's name. Now he's Tiny, CGC.

Obedience trials have been in existence for decades, and Bostons have traditionally excelled at these trials. Bostons have earned the ultimate title of Obedience Trial Champion (OTCh.), a prestigious accomplishment for a dog of any breed.

Obedience trials are held either by themselves or in conjunction with a conformation show. There are essentially three levels, starting with Novice, in which completion of three passing "legs" will earn the dog a Companion Dog (CD) title. The levels then progress in difficulty. Open is the next level, offering the Companion Dog Excellent (CDX) title upon completion of three successful legs. The third level is Utility, which includes off-lead work, silent hand signals and picking the right dumbbells from a group of dumbbells. At this level, successful dogs earn the Utility Dog (UD) title. Not many dogs reach this level, and it is a major accomplishment for both owner and dog when a Utility

degree is achieved. Imagine how proud you'll be to introduce Tiny, UD to your friends! The most elusive title, the OTCh., requires that the dog win three first places under three different judges in the Open B and Utility classes. A rare feat indeed, but there have been a number of Boston Terrier scholars that have become Obedience Trial Champions.

Navigating the agility weave poles is no problem for this bouncy Boston.

Perhaps Tiny, UD can become OTCh. Tiny with a lots of practice and a little luck!

Compared to obedience, which started in the 1930s, competitive agility is a newer sport. Agility began in the 1970s in England and made its way to the US in the 1980s. Agility, most agree, is much more exciting than obedience, since there's a lot of action over various obstacles. Handlers running beside their dogs, with the crowd stirred up and cheering, makes for good doggie fun! Look for the large, noisy ring filled with competitors and dogs running the course, along with excited spectators watching at ringside, joining in with cheers—that's the agility course for certain!

Dogs are taught to run an obstacle course that includes hurdles, ladders, jumps and a variety of other challenges. There are a number of titles in agility, depending upon the obstacles that the dog is able to conquer. AKC defines agility trials as "The enjoyment of bringing together communication, training, timing, accuracy and just plain fun in the ultimate game for you and your dog." It's lots of exercise for both dog and owner, and there is great joy in watching the smart-looking Boston race through his paces! You will find it a pleasure to work agility with your Boston—it's more fun than work!

The ultimate in titles is the Versatile Companion Dog. This is the title that recognizes those dogs and handlers who have been successful in multiple areas of the dog sport. In order to excel at any of the afore-mentioned activities, it is essential to belong to a dog club or training school that has equipment and facilities for practice. You can check